TANZANIAN COOKBOOK

Traditional Recipes from Tanzania

LIAM LUXE

Copyright © 2024 Liam Luxe

All rights reserved.

CONTENTS

INTRODUCTION i
BREAKFAST DELIGHTS 1
    Mandazi (Tanzanian Doughnuts) 1
    Uji (Maize Porridge) 2
    Chapati (Flatbread) with Kachumbari 3
    Nyama Choma (Grilled Meat) Skewers 4
    Zanzibar Spice Omelette 5
    Kaimati (Sweet Dumplings) 6
    Ndizi Kaanga (Fried Plantains) 7
    Vitumbua (Rice Pancakes) 8
    Bhajia (Spiced Potato Fritters) 9
    Maharage Ya Nazi (Coconut Beans) 10
SOUPS AND STEWS 12
    Supu Ya Kuku (Chicken Soup) 12
    Mchuzi Wa Nyama (Beef Stew) 13
    Mchuzi Wa Samaki (Fish Stew) 14
    Supu Ya Maharage (Bean Soup) 16
    Supu Ya Uyoga (Mushroom Soup) 17
    Supu Ya Ndizi (Plantain Soup) 18
    Mtori (Banana and Meat Stew) 19
    Supu Ya Mchicha (Spinach Soup) 21
    Supu Ya Njegere (Green Pea Soup) 22
    Supu Ya Bamia (Okra Soup) 23
VEGETARIAN DELIGHTS 26
    Makande (Coconut Corn) 26

Ugali (Maize Porridge) with Sukuma Wiki 27

Wali Wa Nazi (Coconut Rice) 29

Mchuzi Wa Kunde (Cowpea Stew) 30

Mboga Ya Nazi (Vegetables in Coconut Sauce) 31

Irio (Mashed Vegetables and Peas) 32

Mchuzi Wa Biringanya (Eggplant Stew) 33

Mtori Wa Nazi (Banana and Coconut Stew) 35

Kunde (Cowpeas with Coconut) 36

COASTAL SEAFOOD SPECIALTIES 38

Pweza Wa Kupaka (Coconut Octopus) 38

Samaki Wa Kupaka (Coconut Fish) 40

Ukwaju Wa Nazi (Coconut Crab) 41

Kamba Wa Nazi (Coconut Shrimp) 42

Maharage Ya Nazi Na Kamba (Coconut Beans with Shrimp) 44

Mchuzi Wa Kupaka Kamba (Coconut Sauce with Crab) 45

Supu Ya Kamba (Shrimp Soup) 47

Nyama Ya Ng'ombe Ya Kupaka (Coconut Beef) 48

Mchuzi Wa Kupaka Samaki (Coconut Fish Stew) 50

Mchuzi Wa Kamba Na Maharage (Coconut Shrimp and Beans) 51

GRAINS AND LEGUMES 53

Ugali (Maize Porridge) 53

Wali Wa Nazi (Coconut Rice) 54

Maharage Ya Nazi (Coconut Beans) 55

Ugali Na Mboga Za Majani (Maize Porridge with Greens) 56

Wali Wa Nazi Na Maharage (Coconut Rice and Beans) 57

Kande (Fried Peanuts) 58

Mtori Wa Nazi Na Maharage (Banana and Coconut Stew with Beans)59

Mboga Ya Nazi Na Maharage (Vegetables in Coconut Sauce with Beans) 61

　　Maharage Na Wali (Beans and Rice) 62

　　Kaimati (Sweet Dumplings) 63

SWEET ENDINGS 65

　　Mandazi (Tanzanian Doughnuts) 65

　　Mbatata Wa Nazi (Coconut Sweet Potatoes) 66

　　Kashata (Coconut Candy) 67

　　Mkate Wa Ufuta (Sesame Bread) 68

　　Supu Ya Maboga (Pumpkin Soup) 70

　　Biskuti Ya Nazi (Coconut Cookies) 71

　　Mkate Wa Banana (Banana Bread) 72

MEASUREMENT CONVERSIONS 74

INTRODUCTION

In this cookbook, you'll find yummy Tanzanian dishes that are easy to make at home.
In Tanzania, every dish tells a story about people coming together and sharing their culture. From the busy markets in Dar es Salaam to the tasty smells of Zanzibar, Tanzanian food is a mix of traditions, special ingredients, and cool ways of cooking.
From breakfast treats to soups, seafood, and sweet endings, this book features recipes that capture the heart of Tanzanian cooking. Whether you're a kitchen pro or just starting, these recipes are made for you. Create delicious Tanzanian meals in your own kitchen.
Happy cooking!

BREAKFAST DELIGHTS

MANDAZI (TANZANIAN DOUGHNUTS)

- **Servings:** 12 Mandazis
- **Time:** 30 minutes

Ingredients:

- 2 cups all-purpose flour
- 1/4 cup sugar
- 1 teaspoon baking powder
- 1/4 teaspoon salt
- 1/2 teaspoon ground cinnamon
- 1/2 cup coconut milk
- 1/4 cup water
- Oil for frying

Instructions:

1. In a mixing bowl, combine flour, sugar, baking powder, salt, and cinnamon.
2. Gradually add coconut milk and water, mixing to form a soft dough.
3. Knead the dough on a floured surface until smooth, then let it rest for 10 minutes.
4. Roll out the dough to about 1/2 inch thickness and cut into squares or triangles.
5. Heat oil in a pan over medium heat for frying.
6. Fry Mandazis until golden brown on both sides.
7. Remove from the oil and drain on paper towels.

UJI (MAIZE PORRIDGE)

- **Servings:** 4
- **Time:** 20 minutes

Ingredients:

- 1 cup maize flour
- 4 cups water
- 2 tablespoons sugar (optional)
- Pinch of salt
- 1 cinnamon stick (optional)
- 1/2 cup milk (optional)

Instructions:

1. In a bowl, mix maize flour with 1 cup of water to create a smooth paste.
2. In a saucepan, bring 3 cups of water to a boil.

3. Gradually whisk the maize paste into the boiling water, ensuring no lumps form.
4. Add a pinch of salt and, if desired, a cinnamon stick for flavor.
5. Reduce heat to low and simmer, stirring continuously, until the porridge thickens.
6. If using, add sugar to taste and continue to stir until well combined.
7. Optional: Stir in milk for added creaminess.
8. Remove the cinnamon stick if used, and serve the Uji warm in bowls.

CHAPATI (FLATBREAD) WITH KACHUMBARI

- **Servings:** 8 Chapatis
- **Time:** 45 minutes

Ingredients: For Chapati:

- 2 cups all-purpose flour
- 1 cup water
- 2 tablespoons vegetable oil
- 1/2 teaspoon salt

For Kachumbari:

- 2 tomatoes, diced
- 1 onion, finely chopped
- 1 cucumber, diced
- 1/2 cup fresh cilantro, chopped
- 1 green chili, finely chopped
- Salt to taste

- Lemon juice to taste

Instructions: For Chapati:

1. In a bowl, mix flour and salt. Gradually add water and knead to form a soft dough.
2. Divide the dough into golf ball-sized portions and roll each into a thin, round chapati.
3. Heat a skillet over medium heat. Cook each chapati for 1-2 minutes on each side, applying oil as needed, until golden brown spots appear.

For Kachumbari: 4. In a separate bowl, combine tomatoes, onions, cucumber, cilantro, and green chili.

5. Season with salt and dress with lemon juice according to your taste.

NYAMA CHOMA (GRILLED MEAT) SKEWERS

- **Servings:** 6 Skewers
- **Time:** 30 minutes (plus marination time)

Ingredients:

- 1.5 lbs beef or goat meat, cut into cubes
- 1 onion, finely chopped
- 2 tablespoons vegetable oil
- 2 teaspoons paprika
- 1 teaspoon cayenne pepper (adjust to taste)
- 1 teaspoon ground cumin
- Salt and black pepper to taste

- Wooden skewers, soaked in water

Instructions:

1. In a bowl, combine chopped onions, vegetable oil, paprika, cayenne pepper, ground cumin, salt, and black pepper to create a marinade.
2. Add meat cubes to the marinade, ensuring they are well-coated. Allow it to marinate for at least 2 hours or overnight for richer flavor.
3. Preheat your grill or grill pan over medium-high heat.
4. Thread marinated meat cubes onto the soaked wooden skewers.
5. Grill the skewers for about 10-15 minutes, turning occasionally, until the meat is cooked to your liking.
6. Serve Nyama Choma hot, accompanied by your favorite Tanzanian side dishes or sauces.

ZANZIBAR SPICE OMELETTE

- **Servings:** 2
- **Time:** 15 minutes

Ingredients:

- 4 large eggs
- 1 small onion, finely chopped
- 1 small tomato, diced
- 1/2 teaspoon ground cumin
- 1/2 teaspoon ground coriander
- 1/4 teaspoon turmeric powder
- Salt and pepper to taste
- 2 tablespoons vegetable oil

- Fresh cilantro for garnish (optional)

Instructions:

1. Crack the eggs into a bowl and beat them until well combined.
2. In a separate bowl, mix chopped onion, diced tomato, ground cumin, ground coriander, turmeric powder, salt, and pepper.
3. Heat vegetable oil in a non-stick skillet over medium heat.
4. Pour the beaten eggs into the skillet, tilting it to ensure even distribution.
5. Spoon the spice and vegetable mixture over half of the omelette.
6. Allow the omelette to cook until the edges set, then carefully fold it in half with a spatula.
7. Cook for an additional 2-3 minutes until the omelette is fully cooked and slightly golden.
8. Garnish with fresh cilantro if desired.

KAIMATI (SWEET DUMPLINGS)

- **Servings:** 15-20 dumplings
- **Time:** 45 minutes

Ingredients:

- 2 cups all-purpose flour
- 1/2 cup coconut milk
- 1/4 cup sugar
- 1 teaspoon baking powder
- 1/4 teaspoon ground cardamom

- Oil for deep frying
- 1 cup sugar (for syrup)
- 1/2 cup water (for syrup)
- 1/2 teaspoon lemon juice (for syrup)

Instructions:

1. In a bowl, combine all-purpose flour, coconut milk, sugar, baking powder, and ground cardamom. Mix well to form a smooth dough.
2. Pinch small portions of the dough and roll them into balls or small dumplings.
3. Heat oil in a deep pan over medium heat for frying.
4. Fry the dumplings until they turn golden brown, turning them for even cooking.
5. In a separate saucepan, make a syrup by dissolving sugar in water over low heat. Add lemon juice to prevent crystallization.
6. Dip the fried dumplings into the sugar syrup, ensuring they are well-coated.
7. Remove the sweet dumplings from the syrup and let them cool for a few minutes.

NDIZI KAANGA (FRIED PLANTAINS)

- **Servings:** 4
- **Time:** 15 minutes

Ingredients:

- 4 ripe plantains
- Vegetable oil for frying
- Pinch of salt (optional)

- Honey or powdered sugar for drizzling (optional)

Instructions:

1. Peel the ripe plantains and cut them into diagonal slices or desired shapes.
2. Heat vegetable oil in a frying pan over medium heat.
3. Carefully place the plantain slices into the hot oil, ensuring not to overcrowd the pan.
4. Fry the plantains for 2-3 minutes on each side or until they are golden brown and slightly caramelized.
5. Use a slotted spoon to remove the fried plantains and place them on a paper towel to absorb excess oil.
6. Sprinkle with a pinch of salt if desired.
7. Optional: Drizzle honey or sprinkle powdered sugar over the fried plantains for added sweetness.

VITUMBUA (RICE PANCAKES)

- **Servings:** 12-15 pancakes
- **Time:** 30 minutes (plus soaking time)

Ingredients:

- 1 cup rice
- 1/2 cup coconut milk
- 1/4 cup sugar
- 1/2 teaspoon active dry yeast
- 1/4 teaspoon ground cardamom
- 1/4 teaspoon baking powder
- Oil for greasing the pan

Instructions:

1. Rinse the rice and soak it in water for at least 4 hours or overnight.
2. Drain the soaked rice and blend it into a smooth batter with coconut milk.
3. In a bowl, mix the rice batter, sugar, active dry yeast, ground cardamom, and baking powder. Let it rest for 30 minutes to allow the yeast to activate.
4. Heat a Vitumbua pan or a small round-bottomed skillet over medium heat and lightly grease the molds with oil.
5. Pour a spoonful of batter into each mold, filling them halfway.
6. Cook until the edges start to set and small bubbles form on the surface.
7. Flip each Vitumbua with a skewer or fork to cook the other side until golden brown.
8. Remove from the pan and repeat the process until all the batter is used.

BHAJIA (SPICED POTATO FRITTERS)

- **Servings:** 4
- **Time:** 30 minutes

Ingredients:

- 4 large potatoes, peeled and thinly sliced
- 1 cup chickpea flour (besan)
- 1/2 cup water
- 1 teaspoon ground cumin
- 1 teaspoon ground coriander
- 1/2 teaspoon turmeric powder
- 1/2 teaspoon red chili powder (adjust to taste)
- Salt to taste

- Oil for deep frying
- Fresh coriander leaves for garnish (optional)

Instructions:

1. In a bowl, mix chickpea flour with water to create a smooth, thick batter.
2. Add ground cumin, ground coriander, turmeric powder, red chili powder, and salt to the batter. Stir until well combined.
3. Heat oil in a deep pan over medium heat for frying.
4. Dip each potato slice into the spiced batter, ensuring it's well-coated.
5. Carefully place the coated potato slices into the hot oil, a few at a time.
6. Fry until the Bhajias are golden brown and crisp, turning them for even cooking.
7. Use a slotted spoon to remove the fritters and place them on a paper towel to absorb excess oil.
8. Garnish with fresh coriander leaves if desired.

MAHARAGE YA NAZI (COCONUT BEANS)

- **Servings:** 4
- **Time:** 40 minutes

Ingredients:

- 2 cups cooked red kidney beans
- 1 cup coconut milk
- 1 onion, finely chopped
- 2 tomatoes, diced
- 2 cloves garlic, minced

- 1 teaspoon ground coriander
- 1/2 teaspoon turmeric powder
- 1/2 teaspoon cayenne pepper (adjust to taste)
- Salt to taste
- 2 tablespoons vegetable oil
- Fresh cilantro for garnish (optional)

Instructions:

1. In a pan, heat vegetable oil over medium heat. Add chopped onions and sauté until translucent.
2. Add minced garlic and sauté until fragrant.
3. Stir in ground coriander, turmeric powder, and cayenne pepper. Cook for an additional minute.
4. Add diced tomatoes to the spice mixture and cook until they soften.
5. Pour in the coconut milk, stirring well to combine the ingredients.
6. Add the cooked red kidney beans and salt to the coconut mixture. Simmer for 15-20 minutes, allowing the flavors to meld.
7. Garnish with fresh cilantro if desired.

SOUPS AND STEWS

SUPU YA KUKU (CHICKEN SOUP)

- **Servings:** 6
- **Time:** 1 hour

Ingredients:

- 1 whole chicken, cut into pieces
- 1 onion, finely chopped
- 2 carrots, peeled and sliced
- 2 potatoes, peeled and diced
- 1 cup green beans, chopped
- 2 tomatoes, diced
- 2 cloves garlic, minced
- 1 teaspoon ginger, grated
- 1 teaspoon ground turmeric

- 1 teaspoon ground coriander
- Salt and black pepper to taste
- Fresh parsley for garnish

Instructions:

1. In a large pot, combine the chicken pieces, chopped onion, minced garlic, and grated ginger.
2. Add enough water to cover the chicken and bring to a boil. Skim off any foam that rises to the top.
3. Reduce heat to medium-low and let the chicken simmer for about 30 minutes until it's cooked and tender.
4. Add carrots, potatoes, green beans, tomatoes, ground turmeric, and ground coriander to the pot.
5. Season with salt and black pepper to taste. Continue simmering until the vegetables are tender.
6. Adjust the seasoning if needed and remove from heat.
7. Garnish with fresh parsley before serving.

MCHUZI WA NYAMA (BEEF STEW)

- **Servings:** 4
- **Time:** 1.5 hours

Ingredients:

- 1.5 lbs beef stew meat, cubed
- 1 large onion, finely chopped
- 2 tomatoes, diced
- 3 cloves garlic, minced
- 1 teaspoon ginger, grated
- 2 potatoes, peeled and diced
- 2 carrots, peeled and sliced

- 1 bell pepper, chopped
- 2 tablespoons tomato paste
- 1 teaspoon ground cumin
- 1 teaspoon paprika
- 1 teaspoon curry powder
- Salt and black pepper to taste
- 2 tablespoons vegetable oil
- Fresh cilantro for garnish

Instructions:

1. In a large pot, heat vegetable oil over medium heat. Add chopped onions, minced garlic, and grated ginger. Sauté until onions are translucent.
2. Add beef cubes to the pot and brown them on all sides.
3. Stir in tomato paste, ground cumin, paprika, curry powder, salt, and black pepper. Cook for 2-3 minutes to enhance the flavors.
4. Add diced tomatoes and cook until they break down and release their juices.
5. Pour in enough water to cover the meat, bring to a boil, then reduce heat to low, cover, and simmer for 1 hour or until the meat is tender.
6. Add diced potatoes, sliced carrots, and chopped bell pepper to the stew. Simmer until the vegetables are cooked.
7. Adjust seasoning if needed and let the stew simmer for an additional 15 minutes.
8. Garnish with fresh cilantro before serving.

MCHUZI WA SAMAKI (FISH STEW)

- **Servings:** 4

- **Time:** 45 minutes

Ingredients:

- 1.5 lbs firm fish fillets (such as tilapia or cod), cut into chunks
- 1 onion, finely chopped
- 2 tomatoes, diced
- 3 cloves garlic, minced
- 1 teaspoon ginger, grated
- 1/2 cup coconut milk
- 2 tablespoons tomato paste
- 1 teaspoon ground coriander
- 1 teaspoon ground cumin
- 1/2 teaspoon turmeric powder
- 1/2 teaspoon cayenne pepper (adjust to taste)
- Salt and black pepper to taste
- 2 tablespoons vegetable oil
- Fresh cilantro for garnish

Instructions:

1. In a large pot, heat vegetable oil over medium heat. Add chopped onions, minced garlic, and grated ginger. Sauté until onions are translucent.
2. Stir in tomato paste, ground coriander, ground cumin, turmeric powder, cayenne pepper, salt, and black pepper. Cook for 2-3 minutes.
3. Add diced tomatoes and cook until they break down and form a thick mixture.
4. Place fish chunks into the pot, gently stirring to coat them with the spice mixture.

5. Pour in coconut milk and enough water to cover the fish. Bring to a gentle simmer.
6. Cover the pot and let the stew simmer for about 20-25 minutes or until the fish is cooked through.
7. Adjust seasoning if needed and let the stew simmer for an additional 5 minutes.
8. Garnish with fresh cilantro before serving.

SUPU YA MAHARAGE (BEAN SOUP)

- **Servings:** 6
- **Time:** 1 hour (plus soaking time)

Ingredients:

- 2 cups dried red kidney beans
- 1 onion, finely chopped
- 2 tomatoes, diced
- 3 cloves garlic, minced
- 1 teaspoon ginger, grated
- 1 teaspoon ground coriander
- 1 teaspoon ground cumin
- 1/2 teaspoon turmeric powder
- 1/2 teaspoon cayenne pepper (adjust to taste)
- Salt and black pepper to taste
- 2 tablespoons vegetable oil
- Fresh parsley for garnish

Instructions:

1. Rinse the dried red kidney beans and soak them in water for at least 4 hours or overnight.

2. Drain the soaked beans and place them in a large pot with enough water to cover them. Bring to a boil, then reduce heat and simmer until beans are tender.
3. In a separate pan, heat vegetable oil over medium heat. Add chopped onions, minced garlic, and grated ginger. Sauté until onions are translucent.
4. Stir in ground coriander, ground cumin, turmeric powder, cayenne pepper, salt, and black pepper. Cook for 2-3 minutes.
5. Add diced tomatoes to the spice mixture and cook until they break down and release their juices.
6. Transfer the spice and tomato mixture to the pot of cooked beans. Allow the flavors to meld by simmering for an additional 15-20 minutes.
7. Adjust seasoning if needed and remove from heat.
8. Garnish with fresh parsley before serving.

SUPU YA UYOGA (MUSHROOM SOUP)

- **Servings:** 4
- **Time:** 40 minutes

Ingredients:

- 2 cups fresh mushrooms, sliced
- 1 onion, finely chopped
- 2 cloves garlic, minced
- 1 teaspoon ginger, grated
- 2 tomatoes, diced
- 4 cups vegetable or chicken broth
- 1/2 cup heavy cream (optional)
- 2 tablespoons all-purpose flour
- 2 tablespoons butter

- 1 teaspoon dried thyme
- Salt and black pepper to taste
- Fresh parsley for garnish

Instructions:

1. In a pot, melt butter over medium heat. Add chopped onions, minced garlic, and grated ginger. Sauté until onions are soft and translucent.
2. Add sliced mushrooms to the pot and cook until they release their moisture and become golden brown.
3. Sprinkle flour over the mushrooms and stir to coat, allowing it to cook for 2-3 minutes to eliminate the raw flour taste.
4. Pour in the vegetable or chicken broth, stirring continuously to avoid lumps.
5. Add diced tomatoes and dried thyme to the pot. Bring the soup to a gentle simmer and let it cook for about 15-20 minutes.
6. Optional: Stir in heavy cream for a richer consistency.
7. Season with salt and black pepper to taste.
8. Garnish with fresh parsley before serving.

SUPU YA NDIZI (PLANTAIN SOUP)

- **Servings:** 4
- **Time:** 45 minutes

Ingredients:

- 2 ripe plantains, peeled and sliced
- 1 onion, finely chopped
- 2 tomatoes, diced

- 1 carrot, peeled and sliced
- 2 cloves garlic, minced
- 1 teaspoon ginger, grated
- 4 cups vegetable or chicken broth
- 1 cup coconut milk
- 2 tablespoons vegetable oil
- 1 teaspoon ground cumin
- 1/2 teaspoon ground coriander
- 1/2 teaspoon turmeric powder
- 1/2 teaspoon cayenne pepper (adjust to taste)
- Salt and black pepper to taste
- Fresh cilantro for garnish

Instructions:

1. In a pot, heat vegetable oil over medium heat. Add chopped onions, minced garlic, and grated ginger. Sauté until onions are soft and translucent.
2. Add sliced plantains and cook until they start to soften and caramelize.
3. Stir in ground cumin, ground coriander, turmeric powder, and cayenne pepper. Cook for an additional 2-3 minutes.
4. Add diced tomatoes and sliced carrots to the pot. Cook until the vegetables begin to release their juices.
5. Pour in the vegetable or chicken broth and coconut milk. Bring the soup to a gentle simmer and let it cook for about 20-25 minutes.
6. Season with salt and black pepper to taste.
7. Adjust the consistency by adding more broth if necessary.
8. Garnish with fresh cilantro before serving.

MTORI (BANANA AND MEAT STEW)

- **Servings:** 4
- **Time:** 1.5 hours

Ingredients:

- 1 lb beef or goat meat, cubed
- 2 green bananas, peeled and sliced
- 1 onion, finely chopped
- 2 tomatoes, diced
- 3 cloves garlic, minced
- 1 teaspoon ginger, grated
- 1 cup yogurt
- 2 cups water
- 2 tablespoons vegetable oil
- 1 teaspoon ground coriander
- 1/2 teaspoon ground cinnamon
- 1/2 teaspoon ground cloves
- Salt and black pepper to taste
- Fresh parsley for garnish

Instructions:

1. In a pot, heat vegetable oil over medium heat. Add chopped onions, minced garlic, and grated ginger. Sauté until onions are soft and translucent.
2. Add cubed meat to the pot and brown on all sides.
3. Stir in ground coriander, ground cinnamon, ground cloves, salt, and black pepper. Cook for an additional 2-3 minutes.
4. Add diced tomatoes to the pot and cook until they break down and form a thick mixture.

5. Pour in water and bring the stew to a gentle simmer. Cover and let it cook for about 45 minutes to an hour until the meat is tender.
6. Add sliced green bananas to the stew and continue simmering until the bananas are cooked and the stew thickens.
7. Stir in yogurt and cook for an additional 10 minutes, ensuring the flavors blend well.
8. Adjust seasoning if needed and garnish with fresh parsley before serving.

SUPU YA MCHICHA (SPINACH SOUP)

- **Servings:** 4
- **Time:** 30 minutes

Ingredients:

- 1 bunch fresh spinach, washed and chopped
- 1 onion, finely chopped
- 2 tomatoes, diced
- 2 potatoes, peeled and diced
- 2 cloves garlic, minced
- 1 teaspoon ginger, grated
- 4 cups vegetable or chicken broth
- 2 tablespoons vegetable oil
- 1 teaspoon ground cumin
- 1/2 teaspoon ground coriander
- 1/2 teaspoon turmeric powder
- 1/2 teaspoon cayenne pepper (adjust to taste)
- Salt and black pepper to taste
- Fresh lemon wedges for serving

Instructions:

1. In a pot, heat vegetable oil over medium heat. Add chopped onions, minced garlic, and grated ginger. Sauté until onions are soft and translucent.
2. Add diced tomatoes to the pot and cook until they break down and form a thick mixture.
3. Stir in ground cumin, ground coriander, turmeric powder, and cayenne pepper. Cook for an additional 2-3 minutes.
4. Add diced potatoes and cook until they start to soften.
5. Pour in the vegetable or chicken broth and bring the soup to a gentle simmer. Let it cook for about 15-20 minutes until the potatoes are tender.
6. Add chopped spinach to the pot and cook until it wilts and becomes tender.
7. Season with salt and black pepper to taste.
8. Serve Supu Ya Mchicha hot, with a squeeze of fresh lemon juice for added brightness.

SUPU YA NJEGERE (GREEN PEA SOUP)

- **Servings:** 4
- **Time:** 40 minutes

Ingredients:

- 2 cups green peas (fresh or frozen)
- 1 onion, finely chopped
- 2 potatoes, peeled and diced
- 2 carrots, peeled and sliced
- 2 cloves garlic, minced
- 1 teaspoon ginger, grated

- 4 cups vegetable or chicken broth
- 2 tablespoons vegetable oil
- 1 teaspoon ground cumin
- 1/2 teaspoon ground coriander
- 1/2 teaspoon turmeric powder
- Salt and black pepper to taste
- Fresh mint leaves for garnish

Instructions:

1. In a pot, heat vegetable oil over medium heat. Add chopped onions, minced garlic, and grated ginger. Sauté until onions are soft and translucent.
2. Add diced potatoes and sliced carrots to the pot. Cook until they start to soften.
3. Stir in ground cumin, ground coriander, turmeric powder, salt, and black pepper. Cook for an additional 2-3 minutes.
4. Add green peas to the pot and cook for a few minutes, stirring to combine the flavors.
5. Pour in the vegetable or chicken broth and bring the soup to a gentle simmer. Let it cook for about 20-25 minutes until the vegetables are tender.
6. Adjust seasoning if needed.
7. Using an immersion blender or a regular blender, puree the soup until smooth.
8. Serve Supu Ya Njegere hot, garnished with fresh mint leaves.

SUPU YA BAMIA (OKRA SOUP)

- **Servings:** 4
- **Time:** 40 minutes

Ingredients:

- 1 lb fresh okra, sliced
- 1 onion, finely chopped
- 2 tomatoes, diced
- 2 potatoes, peeled and diced
- 2 cloves garlic, minced
- 1 teaspoon ginger, grated
- 4 cups vegetable or chicken broth
- 2 tablespoons vegetable oil
- 1 teaspoon ground cumin
- 1/2 teaspoon ground coriander
- 1/2 teaspoon turmeric powder
- 1/2 teaspoon cayenne pepper (adjust to taste)
- Salt and black pepper to taste
- Fresh cilantro for garnish

Instructions:

1. In a pot, heat vegetable oil over medium heat. Add chopped onions, minced garlic, and grated ginger. Sauté until onions are soft and translucent.
2. Add diced potatoes to the pot and cook until they start to soften.
3. Stir in ground cumin, ground coriander, turmeric powder, and cayenne pepper. Cook for an additional 2-3 minutes.
4. Add sliced okra to the pot and cook for a few minutes until it begins to soften.
5. Add diced tomatoes and cook until they break down and form a thick mixture.

6. Pour in the vegetable or chicken broth and bring the soup to a gentle simmer. Let it cook for about 20-25 minutes until the vegetables are tender.
7. Season with salt and black pepper to taste.
8. Serve Supu Ya Bamia hot, garnished with fresh cilantro.

VEGETARIAN DELIGHTS

MAKANDE (COCONUT CORN)

- **Servings:** 4
- **Time:** 30 minutes

Ingredients:

- 2 cups fresh or frozen corn kernels
- 1 cup coconut milk
- 1 onion, finely chopped
- 2 tomatoes, diced
- 2 tablespoons vegetable oil
- 2 cloves garlic, minced
- 1 teaspoon ginger, grated
- 1 teaspoon ground coriander
- 1/2 teaspoon ground cumin

- 1/2 teaspoon turmeric powder
- 1/2 teaspoon cayenne pepper (adjust to taste)
- Salt to taste
- Fresh cilantro for garnish

Instructions:

1. In a pan, heat vegetable oil over medium heat. Add chopped onions, minced garlic, and grated ginger. Sauté until onions are soft and translucent.
2. Add diced tomatoes to the pan and cook until they break down and form a thick mixture.
3. Stir in ground coriander, ground cumin, turmeric powder, cayenne pepper, and salt. Cook for an additional 2-3 minutes.
4. Add corn kernels to the pan and mix well with the spice and tomato mixture.
5. Pour in coconut milk, stirring to combine all the ingredients. Allow the mixture to simmer for 15-20 minutes until the corn is cooked and the flavors meld.
6. Adjust seasoning if needed.
7. Garnish with fresh cilantro before serving.

UGALI (MAIZE PORRIDGE) WITH SUKUMA WIKI

- **Servings:** 4
- **Time:** 30 minutes

Ugali (Maize Porridge):

Ingredients:

- 1 cup maize flour (cornmeal)
- 2 cups water
- Salt to taste

Instructions:

1. In a pot, bring 2 cups of water to a boil.
2. Gradually add maize flour to the boiling water, stirring continuously to avoid lumps.
3. Continue stirring until the mixture thickens and forms a smooth, consistent porridge.
4. Reduce the heat to low and cover the pot. Allow the Ugali to cook for an additional 10-15 minutes until it reaches a thick consistency.
5. Add salt to taste and continue stirring to combine.

Sukuma Wiki:

Ingredients:

- 1 bunch sukuma wiki (collard greens), finely chopped
- 1 onion, finely chopped
- 2 tomatoes, diced
- 2 tablespoons vegetable oil
- 2 cloves garlic, minced
- 1 teaspoon ground cumin
- Salt and black pepper to taste

Instructions:

1. In a pan, heat vegetable oil over medium heat. Add chopped onions and minced garlic. Sauté until onions are soft and translucent.

2. Add diced tomatoes to the pan and cook until they break down and form a thick mixture.
3. Stir in ground cumin, salt, and black pepper. Cook for an additional 2-3 minutes.
4. Add finely chopped sukuma wiki to the pan, mixing well with the spice and tomato mixture. Cook until the greens are wilted and tender.

WALI WA NAZI (COCONUT RICE)

- **Servings:** 4
- **Time:** 25 minutes

Ingredients:

- 2 cups basmati rice
- 1 cup coconut milk
- 1 cup water
- 1 onion, finely chopped
- 2 tablespoons vegetable oil
- 2 cloves garlic, minced
- 1 teaspoon ginger, grated
- 1 cinnamon stick
- 3 cardamom pods
- Salt to taste
- Fresh cilantro for garnish (optional)

Instructions:

1. Rinse the basmati rice under cold water until the water runs clear. Drain any excess water.

2. In a pot, heat vegetable oil over medium heat. Add chopped onions, minced garlic, and grated ginger. Sauté until onions are soft and translucent.
3. Add the basmati rice to the pot, stirring to coat the rice with the aromatic onion mixture.
4. Pour in coconut milk and water, and add the cinnamon stick and cardamom pods. Stir well to combine.
5. Bring the mixture to a boil, then reduce heat to low, cover the pot, and let it simmer for 15-20 minutes until the rice is cooked and has absorbed the liquid.
6. Add salt to taste and fluff the rice with a fork to separate the grains.
7. Optional: Garnish with fresh cilantro before serving.

MCHUZI WA KUNDE (COWPEA STEW)

- **Servings:** 4
- **Time:** 40 minutes

Ingredients:

- 2 cups cowpeas (black-eyed peas), soaked and cooked
- 1 onion, finely chopped
- 2 tomatoes, diced
- 2 tablespoons vegetable oil
- 2 cloves garlic, minced
- 1 teaspoon ginger, grated
- 1 teaspoon ground coriander
- 1/2 teaspoon ground cumin
- 1/2 teaspoon turmeric powder
- 1/2 teaspoon cayenne pepper (adjust to taste)
- Salt to taste
- Fresh coriander leaves for garnish

Instructions:

1. In a pan, heat vegetable oil over medium heat. Add chopped onions, minced garlic, and grated ginger. Sauté until onions are soft and translucent.
2. Add diced tomatoes to the pan and cook until they break down and form a thick mixture.
3. Stir in ground coriander, ground cumin, turmeric powder, and cayenne pepper. Cook for an additional 2-3 minutes.
4. Add cooked cowpeas to the pan, mixing well with the spice and tomato mixture.
5. Pour in enough water to achieve your desired consistency for the stew.
6. Season with salt to taste and let the stew simmer for 15-20 minutes to allow the flavors to meld.
7. Adjust seasoning if needed.
8. Garnish with fresh coriander leaves before serving.

MBOGA YA NAZI (VEGETABLES IN COCONUT SAUCE)

- **Servings:** 4
- **Time:** 30 minutes

Ingredients:

- 2 cups mixed vegetables (e.g., carrots, green beans, peas), chopped
- 1 onion, finely chopped
- 1 cup coconut milk
- 2 tablespoons vegetable oil
- 2 cloves garlic, minced

- 1 teaspoon ginger, grated
- 1 teaspoon ground coriander
- 1/2 teaspoon ground cumin
- 1/2 teaspoon turmeric powder
- 1/2 teaspoon cayenne pepper (adjust to taste)
- Salt to taste
- Fresh cilantro for garnish

Instructions:

1. In a pan, heat vegetable oil over medium heat. Add chopped onions, minced garlic, and grated ginger. Sauté until onions are soft and translucent.
2. Add mixed vegetables to the pan and cook until they are slightly tender.
3. Stir in ground coriander, ground cumin, turmeric powder, and cayenne pepper. Cook for an additional 2-3 minutes.
4. Pour in coconut milk, stirring well to coat the vegetables with the flavorful mixture.
5. Season with salt to taste and let the vegetables simmer in the coconut sauce for 15-20 minutes until they are fully cooked and absorb the flavors.
6. Adjust seasoning if needed.
7. Garnish with fresh cilantro before serving.

IRIO (MASHED VEGETABLES AND PEAS)

- **Servings:** 4
- **Time:** 40 minutes

Ingredients:

- 2 cups green peas
- 4 medium potatoes, peeled and diced
- 2 cups fresh maize kernels (corn)
- 1 cup fresh green beans, chopped
- 1 onion, finely chopped
- 2 tablespoons vegetable oil
- 2 tablespoons unsalted butter
- Salt to taste
- Black pepper to taste

Instructions:

1. In a pot, bring water to a boil. Add green peas and cook for about 5 minutes until they are tender. Drain and set aside.
2. In a separate pot, boil potatoes until they are fork-tender.
3. In another pot, cook fresh maize kernels and green beans until they are tender. Drain any excess water.
4. In a pan, heat vegetable oil over medium heat. Add chopped onions and sauté until they are soft and translucent.
5. Mash the boiled potatoes in a large bowl.
6. Add the cooked green peas, maize kernels, and green beans to the mashed potatoes. Mix well.
7. Incorporate unsalted butter into the mixture, ensuring it melts evenly.
8. Season with salt and black pepper to taste. Continue to mash and mix until you achieve a uniform consistency.

MCHUZI WA BIRINGANYA (EGGPLANT STEW)

- **Servings:** 4
- **Time:** 40 minutes

Ingredients:

- 2 medium-sized eggplants, diced
- 1 onion, finely chopped
- 2 tomatoes, diced
- 2 tablespoons vegetable oil
- 2 cloves garlic, minced
- 1 teaspoon ginger, grated
- 1 teaspoon ground coriander
- 1/2 teaspoon ground cumin
- 1/2 teaspoon turmeric powder
- 1/2 teaspoon cayenne pepper (adjust to taste)
- Salt to taste
- Fresh cilantro for garnish

Instructions:

1. In a pan, heat vegetable oil over medium heat. Add chopped onions, minced garlic, and grated ginger. Sauté until onions are soft and translucent.
2. Add diced eggplants to the pan and cook until they are slightly tender.
3. Stir in ground coriander, ground cumin, turmeric powder, and cayenne pepper. Cook for an additional 2-3 minutes.
4. Add diced tomatoes to the pan and cook until they break down and form a thick mixture.
5. Pour in a little water to achieve your desired stew consistency. Allow the stew to simmer for 15-20 minutes

until the eggplants are fully cooked and absorb the flavors.
6. Season with salt to taste.
7. Garnish with fresh cilantro before serving.

MTORI WA NAZI (BANANA AND COCONUT STEW)

- **Servings:** 4
- **Time:** 1 hour

Ingredients:

- 4 ripe bananas, peeled and sliced
- 1 cup grated coconut
- 1 onion, finely chopped
- 2 tomatoes, diced
- 1 cup yogurt
- 2 tablespoons vegetable oil
- 2 cloves garlic, minced
- 1 teaspoon ginger, grated
- 1 teaspoon ground coriander
- 1/2 teaspoon ground cinnamon
- 1/2 teaspoon ground cloves
- Salt to taste
- Fresh parsley for garnish

Instructions:

1. In a pan, heat vegetable oil over medium heat. Add chopped onions, minced garlic, and grated ginger. Sauté until onions are soft and translucent.

2. Add grated coconut to the pan and toast it for a few minutes until it turns golden brown and releases its aroma.
3. Stir in ground coriander, ground cinnamon, ground cloves, and salt. Cook for an additional 2-3 minutes.
4. Add diced tomatoes to the pan and cook until they break down and form a thick mixture.
5. Add sliced bananas to the pan, gently stirring to coat them with the spice and coconut mixture.
6. Pour in yogurt, ensuring it's well incorporated into the stew.
7. Cover the pan and let the stew simmer for about 30-40 minutes until the bananas are tender and the flavors meld.
8. Adjust seasoning if needed and garnish with fresh parsley before serving.

KUNDE (COWPEAS WITH COCONUT)

- **Servings:** 4
- **Time:** 40 minutes

Ingredients:

- 2 cups cowpeas (black-eyed peas), soaked and cooked
- 1 cup grated coconut
- 1 onion, finely chopped
- 2 tomatoes, diced
- 2 tablespoons vegetable oil
- 2 cloves garlic, minced
- 1 teaspoon ginger, grated
- 1 teaspoon ground coriander
- 1/2 teaspoon ground cumin

- 1/2 teaspoon turmeric powder
- 1/2 teaspoon cayenne pepper (adjust to taste)
- Salt to taste
- Fresh coriander leaves for garnish

Instructions:

1. In a pan, heat vegetable oil over medium heat. Add chopped onions, minced garlic, and grated ginger. Sauté until onions are soft and translucent.
2. Add grated coconut to the pan and toast it for a few minutes until it turns golden brown and releases its aroma.
3. Stir in ground coriander, ground cumin, turmeric powder, and cayenne pepper. Cook for an additional 2-3 minutes.
4. Add cooked cowpeas to the pan, mixing well with the spice and coconut mixture.
5. Add diced tomatoes to the pan and cook until they break down and form a thick mixture.
6. Pour in enough water to achieve your desired consistency for the dish. Allow the mixture to simmer for 15-20 minutes to let the flavors meld.
7. Season with salt to taste and let it simmer for a few more minutes.
8. Garnish with fresh coriander leaves before serving.

COASTAL SEAFOOD SPECIALTIES

PWEZA WA KUPAKA (COCONUT OCTOPUS)

- **Servings:** 4
- **Time:** 1.5 hours (including marination)

Ingredients:

- 1 kg octopus, cleaned and tenderized
- 1 cup coconut milk
- 1 onion, finely chopped
- 2 tomatoes, diced
- 2 tablespoons vegetable oil
- 2 cloves garlic, minced
- 1 teaspoon ginger, grated
- 1 teaspoon ground coriander

- 1/2 teaspoon ground cumin
- 1/2 teaspoon turmeric powder
- 1/2 teaspoon cayenne pepper (adjust to taste)
- Salt to taste
- Fresh cilantro for garnish

Marination:

- Juice of 1 lemon
- 1 teaspoon paprika
- Salt and black pepper to taste

Instructions:

1. Clean and tenderize the octopus. If using fresh octopus, ensure it is properly cleaned and scored to help tenderize the meat.
2. In a bowl, mix the marination ingredients—lemon juice, paprika, salt, and black pepper. Rub the octopus with this mixture and let it marinate for at least 30 minutes.
3. In a pan, heat vegetable oil over medium heat. Add chopped onions, minced garlic, and grated ginger. Sauté until onions are soft and translucent.
4. Add diced tomatoes to the pan and cook until they break down and form a thick mixture.
5. Stir in ground coriander, ground cumin, turmeric powder, and cayenne pepper. Cook for an additional 2-3 minutes.
6. Add the marinated octopus to the pan, pouring coconut milk over it. Ensure the octopus is well-coated with the spice and coconut mixture.
7. Cover the pan and let the octopus simmer for about 1 hour or until it is tender.

8. Season with salt to taste.
9. Garnish with fresh cilantro before serving.

SAMAKI WA KUPAKA (COCONUT FISH)

- **Servings:** 4
- **Time:** 40 minutes

Ingredients:

- 4 fish fillets (snapper, tilapia, or your choice)
- 1 cup coconut milk
- 1 onion, finely chopped
- 2 tomatoes, diced
- 2 tablespoons vegetable oil
- 2 cloves garlic, minced
- 1 teaspoon ginger, grated
- 1 teaspoon ground coriander
- 1/2 teaspoon ground cumin
- 1/2 teaspoon turmeric powder
- 1/2 teaspoon cayenne pepper (adjust to taste)
- Salt to taste
- Fresh cilantro for garnish

Instructions:

1. Clean and pat dry the fish fillets. Make small slits on both sides to allow the flavors to penetrate.
2. In a pan, heat vegetable oil over medium heat. Add chopped onions, minced garlic, and grated ginger. Sauté until onions are soft and translucent.
3. Add diced tomatoes to the pan and cook until they break down and form a thick mixture.

4. Stir in ground coriander, ground cumin, turmeric powder, and cayenne pepper. Cook for an additional 2-3 minutes.
5. Place the fish fillets in the pan, ensuring they are well-coated with the spice and tomato mixture.
6. Pour coconut milk over the fish, ensuring it covers the fillets.
7. Cover the pan and let the fish simmer for about 20-25 minutes or until it is cooked through and flakes easily.
8. Season with salt to taste.
9. Garnish with fresh cilantro before serving.

UKWAJU WA NAZI (COCONUT CRAB)

- **Servings:** 4
- **Time:** 1.5 hours (including marination)

Ingredients:

- 2 crabs, cleaned and cracked
- 1 cup coconut milk
- 1 onion, finely chopped
- 2 tomatoes, diced
- 2 tablespoons vegetable oil
- 2 cloves garlic, minced
- 1 teaspoon ginger, grated
- 1 teaspoon ground coriander
- 1/2 teaspoon ground cumin
- 1/2 teaspoon turmeric powder
- 1/2 teaspoon cayenne pepper (adjust to taste)
- Salt to taste
- Fresh cilantro for garnish

Marination:

- Juice of 1 lime
- 1 teaspoon paprika
- Salt and black pepper to taste

Instructions:

1. Clean and crack the crabs, ensuring they are ready for cooking.
2. In a bowl, mix the marination ingredients—lime juice, paprika, salt, and black pepper. Rub the crabs with this mixture and let them marinate for at least 30 minutes.
3. In a pan, heat vegetable oil over medium heat. Add chopped onions, minced garlic, and grated ginger. Sauté until onions are soft and translucent.
4. Add diced tomatoes to the pan and cook until they break down and form a thick mixture.
5. Stir in ground coriander, ground cumin, turmeric powder, and cayenne pepper. Cook for an additional 2-3 minutes.
6. Place the marinated crabs in the pan, ensuring they are well-coated with the spice and tomato mixture.
7. Pour coconut milk over the crabs, ensuring they are submerged in the flavorful liquid.
8. Cover the pan and let the crabs simmer for about 1 hour or until they are fully cooked and infused with the coconut and spice flavors.
9. Season with salt to taste.
10. Garnish with fresh cilantro before serving.

KAMBA WA NAZI (COCONUT SHRIMP)

- **Servings:** 4
- **Time:** 30 minutes

Ingredients:

- 1 lb shrimp, peeled and deveined
- 1 cup coconut milk
- 1 onion, finely chopped
- 2 tomatoes, diced
- 2 tablespoons vegetable oil
- 2 cloves garlic, minced
- 1 teaspoon ginger, grated
- 1 teaspoon ground coriander
- 1/2 teaspoon ground cumin
- 1/2 teaspoon turmeric powder
- 1/2 teaspoon cayenne pepper (adjust to taste)
- Salt to taste
- Fresh cilantro for garnish
- Lime wedges for serving

Instructions:

1. In a pan, heat vegetable oil over medium heat. Add chopped onions, minced garlic, and grated ginger. Sauté until onions are soft and translucent.
2. Add diced tomatoes to the pan and cook until they break down and form a thick mixture.
3. Stir in ground coriander, ground cumin, turmeric powder, and cayenne pepper. Cook for an additional 2-3 minutes.
4. Add shrimp to the pan, ensuring they are well-coated with the spice and tomato mixture.

5. Pour coconut milk over the shrimp, ensuring they are submerged in the flavorful liquid.
6. Cover the pan and let the shrimp simmer for about 10-15 minutes or until they are pink and cooked through.
7. Season with salt to taste.
8. Garnish with fresh cilantro and serve with lime wedges on the side.

MAHARAGE YA NAZI NA KAMBA (COCONUT BEANS WITH SHRIMP)

- **Servings:** 4
- **Time:** 40 minutes

Ingredients:

- 2 cups cooked beans (black-eyed peas or kidney beans)
- 1 cup shrimp, peeled and deveined
- 1 cup coconut milk
- 1 onion, finely chopped
- 2 tomatoes, diced
- 2 tablespoons vegetable oil
- 2 cloves garlic, minced
- 1 teaspoon ginger, grated
- 1 teaspoon ground coriander
- 1/2 teaspoon ground cumin
- 1/2 teaspoon turmeric powder
- 1/2 teaspoon cayenne pepper (adjust to taste)
- Salt to taste
- Fresh cilantro for garnish
- Lime wedges for serving

Instructions:

1. In a pan, heat vegetable oil over medium heat. Add chopped onions, minced garlic, and grated ginger. Sauté until onions are soft and translucent.
2. Add diced tomatoes to the pan and cook until they break down and form a thick mixture.
3. Stir in ground coriander, ground cumin, turmeric powder, and cayenne pepper. Cook for an additional 2-3 minutes.
4. Add shrimp to the pan, ensuring they are well-coated with the spice and tomato mixture.
5. Pour coconut milk over the shrimp, ensuring they are submerged in the flavorful liquid.
6. Allow the shrimp to cook for about 5-7 minutes until they are pink and cooked through.
7. Add the cooked beans to the pan, mixing well with the shrimp and coconut mixture.
8. Season with salt to taste.
9. Cover the pan and let the dish simmer for an additional 10-15 minutes to allow the flavors to meld.
10. Garnish with fresh cilantro and serve with lime wedges on the side.

MCHUZI WA KUPAKA KAMBA (COCONUT SAUCE WITH CRAB)

- **Servings:** 4
- **Time:** 1.5 hours (including marination)

Ingredients:

- 2 crabs, cleaned and cracked
- 1 cup coconut milk

- 1 onion, finely chopped
- 2 tomatoes, diced
- 2 tablespoons vegetable oil
- 2 cloves garlic, minced
- 1 teaspoon ginger, grated
- 1 teaspoon ground coriander
- 1/2 teaspoon ground cumin
- 1/2 teaspoon turmeric powder
- 1/2 teaspoon cayenne pepper (adjust to taste)
- Salt to taste
- Fresh cilantro for garnish

Marination:

- Juice of 1 lime
- 1 teaspoon paprika
- Salt and black pepper to taste

Instructions:

1. Clean and crack the crabs, ensuring they are ready for cooking.
2. In a bowl, mix the marination ingredients—lime juice, paprika, salt, and black pepper. Rub the crabs with this mixture and let them marinate for at least 30 minutes.
3. In a pan, heat vegetable oil over medium heat. Add chopped onions, minced garlic, and grated ginger. Sauté until onions are soft and translucent.
4. Add diced tomatoes to the pan and cook until they break down and form a thick mixture.
5. Stir in ground coriander, ground cumin, turmeric powder, and cayenne pepper. Cook for an additional 2-3 minutes.

6. Place the marinated crabs in the pan, ensuring they are well-coated with the spice and tomato mixture.
7. Pour coconut milk over the crabs, ensuring they are submerged in the flavorful liquid.
8. Cover the pan and let the crabs simmer for about 1 hour or until they are fully cooked and infused with the coconut and spice flavors.
9. Season with salt to taste.
10. Garnish with fresh cilantro before serving.

SUPU YA KAMBA (SHRIMP SOUP)

- **Servings:** 4
- **Time:** 30 minutes

Ingredients:

- 1 cup shrimp, peeled and deveined
- 1 onion, finely chopped
- 2 tomatoes, diced
- 1 cup coconut milk
- 4 cups fish or vegetable broth
- 2 tablespoons vegetable oil
- 2 cloves garlic, minced
- 1 teaspoon ginger, grated
- 1 teaspoon ground coriander
- 1/2 teaspoon ground cumin
- 1/2 teaspoon turmeric powder
- 1/2 teaspoon cayenne pepper (adjust to taste)
- Salt to taste
- Fresh cilantro for garnish
- Lime wedges for serving

Instructions:

1. In a pot, heat vegetable oil over medium heat. Add chopped onions, minced garlic, and grated ginger. Sauté until onions are soft and translucent.
2. Add diced tomatoes to the pot and cook until they break down and form a thick mixture.
3. Stir in ground coriander, ground cumin, turmeric powder, and cayenne pepper. Cook for an additional 2-3 minutes.
4. Add shrimp to the pot, ensuring they are well-coated with the spice and tomato mixture.
5. Pour in coconut milk and fish or vegetable broth. Stir well to combine.
6. Bring the soup to a gentle simmer and let it cook for about 10-15 minutes until the shrimp are pink and fully cooked.
7. Season with salt to taste.
8. Garnish with fresh cilantro and serve hot with lime wedges on the side.

NYAMA YA NG'OMBE YA KUPAKA (COCONUT BEEF)

- **Servings:** 4
- **Time:** 1.5 hours (including marination)

Ingredients:

- 500g beef, thinly sliced
- 1 cup coconut milk
- 1 onion, finely chopped
- 2 tomatoes, diced

- 2 tablespoons vegetable oil
- 2 cloves garlic, minced
- 1 teaspoon ginger, grated
- 1 teaspoon ground coriander
- 1/2 teaspoon ground cumin
- 1/2 teaspoon turmeric powder
- 1/2 teaspoon cayenne pepper (adjust to taste)
- Salt to taste
- Fresh cilantro for garnish

Marination:

- Juice of 1 lemon
- 1 teaspoon paprika
- Salt and black pepper to taste

Instructions:

1. Thinly slice the beef and place it in a bowl. Mix in the marination ingredients—lemon juice, paprika, salt, and black pepper. Let it marinate for at least 30 minutes.
2. In a pan, heat vegetable oil over medium heat. Add chopped onions, minced garlic, and grated ginger. Sauté until onions are soft and translucent.
3. Add diced tomatoes to the pan and cook until they break down and form a thick mixture.
4. Stir in ground coriander, ground cumin, turmeric powder, and cayenne pepper. Cook for an additional 2-3 minutes.
5. Add the marinated beef to the pan, ensuring it is well-coated with the spice and tomato mixture.
6. Pour coconut milk over the beef, ensuring it is submerged in the flavorful liquid.

7. Cover the pan and let the beef simmer for about 1 hour or until it is tender and infused with the coconut and spice flavors.
8. Season with salt to taste.
9. Garnish with fresh cilantro before serving.

MCHUZI WA KUPAKA SAMAKI (COCONUT FISH STEW)

- **Servings:** 4
- **Time:** 40 minutes

Ingredients:

- 4 fish fillets (snapper, tilapia, or your choice)
- 1 cup coconut milk
- 1 onion, finely chopped
- 2 tomatoes, diced
- 2 tablespoons vegetable oil
- 2 cloves garlic, minced
- 1 teaspoon ginger, grated
- 1 teaspoon ground coriander
- 1/2 teaspoon ground cumin
- 1/2 teaspoon turmeric powder
- 1/2 teaspoon cayenne pepper (adjust to taste)
- Salt to taste
- Fresh cilantro for garnish

Instructions:

1. Clean and pat dry the fish fillets. Make small slits on both sides to allow the flavors to penetrate.

2. In a pan, heat vegetable oil over medium heat. Add chopped onions, minced garlic, and grated ginger. Sauté until onions are soft and translucent.
3. Add diced tomatoes to the pan and cook until they break down and form a thick mixture.
4. Stir in ground coriander, ground cumin, turmeric powder, and cayenne pepper. Cook for an additional 2-3 minutes.
5. Place the fish fillets in the pan, ensuring they are well-coated with the spice and tomato mixture.
6. Pour coconut milk over the fish, ensuring it covers the fillets.
7. Cover the pan and let the fish simmer for about 20-25 minutes or until it is cooked through and flakes easily.
8. Season with salt to taste.
9. Garnish with fresh cilantro before serving.

MCHUZI WA KAMBA NA MAHARAGE (COCONUT SHRIMP AND BEANS)

- **Servings:** 4
- **Time:** 40 minutes

Ingredients:

- 1 cup shrimp, peeled and deveined
- 2 cups cooked beans (black-eyed peas or kidney beans)
- 1 cup coconut milk
- 1 onion, finely chopped
- 2 tomatoes, diced
- 2 tablespoons vegetable oil
- 2 cloves garlic, minced

- 1 teaspoon ginger, grated
- 1 teaspoon ground coriander
- 1/2 teaspoon ground cumin
- 1/2 teaspoon turmeric powder
- 1/2 teaspoon cayenne pepper (adjust to taste)
- Salt to taste
- Fresh cilantro for garnish
- Lime wedges for serving

Instructions:

1. In a pan, heat vegetable oil over medium heat. Add chopped onions, minced garlic, and grated ginger. Sauté until onions are soft and translucent.
2. Add diced tomatoes to the pan and cook until they break down and form a thick mixture.
3. Stir in ground coriander, ground cumin, turmeric powder, and cayenne pepper. Cook for an additional 2-3 minutes.
4. Add shrimp to the pan, ensuring they are well-coated with the spice and tomato mixture.
5. Pour coconut milk over the shrimp, ensuring they are submerged in the flavorful liquid.
6. Allow the shrimp to cook for about 5-7 minutes until they are pink and cooked through.
7. Add the cooked beans to the pan, mixing well with the shrimp and coconut mixture.
8. Season with salt to taste.
9. Cover the pan and let the dish simmer for an additional 10-15 minutes to allow the flavors to meld.
10. Garnish with fresh cilantro and serve with lime wedges on the side.

TANZANIAN COOKBOOK

GRAINS AND LEGUMES

UGALI (MAIZE PORRIDGE)

- **Servings:** 4
- **Time:** 20 minutes

Ingredients:

- 2 cups maize flour (cornmeal)
- 4 cups water
- Salt to taste

Instructions:

1. In a large pot, bring 4 cups of water to a boil.
2. Gradually add the maize flour to the boiling water, stirring continuously to prevent lumps from forming.

3. Reduce the heat to low and continue stirring the mixture until it thickens to a smooth and consistent porridge-like texture.
4. Cover the pot and let it simmer for an additional 10-15 minutes, allowing the maize flour to fully cook.
5. Season with salt to taste and stir well.
6. Once the Ugali reaches a thick, dough-like consistency and easily pulls away from the sides of the pot, it is ready to be served.

WALI WA NAZI (COCONUT RICE)

- **Servings:** 4
- **Time:** 30 minutes

Ingredients:

- 2 cups basmati rice, washed and drained
- 1 cup coconut milk
- 1 cup water
- 1 onion, finely chopped
- 2 tablespoons vegetable oil
- 2 cloves garlic, minced
- 1 teaspoon ginger, grated
- 1 teaspoon ground coriander
- 1/2 teaspoon turmeric powder
- Salt to taste
- Fresh cilantro for garnish

Instructions:

1. In a pot, heat vegetable oil over medium heat. Add chopped onions, minced garlic, and grated ginger. Sauté until onions are soft and translucent.
2. Add ground coriander and turmeric powder to the pot. Stir well to coat the onions in the spices.
3. Add the washed basmati rice to the pot, stirring to combine with the onion and spice mixture.
4. Pour in coconut milk and water, ensuring the rice is well-submerged in the liquid.
5. Season with salt to taste and bring the mixture to a boil.
6. Once boiling, reduce the heat to low, cover the pot, and let the rice simmer for 15-20 minutes or until the rice is tender and has absorbed the coconut-infused flavors.
7. Fluff the rice with a fork to separate the grains.
8. Garnish with fresh cilantro before serving.

MAHARAGE YA NAZI (COCONUT BEANS)

- **Servings:** 4
- **Time:** 40 minutes

Ingredients:

- 2 cups cooked beans (black-eyed peas or kidney beans)
- 1 cup coconut milk
- 1 onion, finely chopped
- 2 tomatoes, diced
- 2 tablespoons vegetable oil
- 2 cloves garlic, minced
- 1 teaspoon ginger, grated
- 1 teaspoon ground coriander
- 1/2 teaspoon turmeric powder
- 1/2 teaspoon cayenne pepper (adjust to taste)

- Salt to taste
- Fresh cilantro for garnish

Instructions:

1. In a pan, heat vegetable oil over medium heat. Add chopped onions, minced garlic, and grated ginger. Sauté until onions are soft and translucent.
2. Add diced tomatoes to the pan and cook until they break down and form a thick mixture.
3. Stir in ground coriander, turmeric powder, and cayenne pepper. Cook for an additional 2-3 minutes.
4. Add cooked beans to the pan, mixing well with the spice and tomato mixture.
5. Pour coconut milk over the beans, ensuring they are well-coated with the flavorful liquid.
6. Season with salt to taste and allow the mixture to simmer for 15-20 minutes, letting the flavors meld.
7. Garnish with fresh cilantro before serving.

UGALI NA MBOGA ZA MAJANI (MAIZE PORRIDGE WITH GREENS)

- **Servings:** 4
- **Time:** 30 minutes

Ingredients:

- 2 cups maize flour (cornmeal)
- 4 cups water
- Salt to taste
- Assorted leafy greens (spinach, collard greens, kale), washed and chopped

Instructions:

1. In a large pot, bring 4 cups of water to a boil.
2. Gradually add the maize flour to the boiling water, stirring continuously to prevent lumps from forming.
3. Reduce the heat to low and continue stirring the mixture until it thickens to a smooth and consistent porridge-like texture.
4. Add salt to taste and stir well.
5. Toss in the chopped leafy greens, mixing them into the porridge until they are evenly distributed.
6. Cover the pot and let the mixture simmer for an additional 10-15 minutes, allowing the maize flour to fully cook and the greens to wilt.
7. Once the Ugali reaches a thick, dough-like consistency and the greens are tender, it is ready to be served.

WALI WA NAZI NA MAHARAGE (COCONUT RICE AND BEANS)

- **Servings:** 4
- **Time:** 40 minutes

Ingredients:

- 2 cups basmati rice, washed and drained
- 1 cup cooked beans (black-eyed peas or kidney beans)
- 1 cup coconut milk
- 1 onion, finely chopped
- 2 tomatoes, diced
- 2 tablespoons vegetable oil
- 2 cloves garlic, minced
- 1 teaspoon ginger, grated

- 1 teaspoon ground coriander
- 1/2 teaspoon turmeric powder
- 1/2 teaspoon cayenne pepper (adjust to taste)
- Salt to taste
- Fresh cilantro for garnish

Instructions:

1. In a pot, heat vegetable oil over medium heat. Add chopped onions, minced garlic, and grated ginger. Sauté until onions are soft and translucent.
2. Add diced tomatoes to the pot and cook until they break down and form a thick mixture.
3. Stir in ground coriander, turmeric powder, and cayenne pepper. Cook for an additional 2-3 minutes.
4. Add cooked beans to the pot, mixing well with the spice and tomato mixture.
5. Add washed basmati rice to the pot, stirring to combine with the other ingredients.
6. Pour in coconut milk, ensuring the rice and beans are well-submerged in the liquid.
7. Season with salt to taste and bring the mixture to a boil.
8. Once boiling, reduce the heat to low, cover the pot, and let the rice simmer for 15-20 minutes or until the rice is tender and has absorbed the coconut-infused flavors.
9. Fluff the rice with a fork to separate the grains.
10. Garnish with fresh cilantro before serving.

KANDE (FRIED PEANUTS)

- **Servings:** 4
- **Time:** 15 minutes

Ingredients:

- 2 cups raw peanuts, shelled
- 2 tablespoons vegetable oil
- Salt to taste
- Optional: Chili powder or paprika for added spice

Instructions:

1. In a pan, heat vegetable oil over medium heat.
2. Add the shelled peanuts to the pan, ensuring they are in a single layer.
3. Stir the peanuts frequently to prevent burning and promote even cooking.
4. Continue frying the peanuts until they turn golden brown and emit a nutty aroma. This usually takes about 10-12 minutes.
5. Once fried to your desired level of crispiness, remove the peanuts from the pan.
6. Sprinkle salt over the hot peanuts and toss them to coat evenly. Adjust salt to taste.
7. Optional: If you enjoy spiciness, sprinkle chili powder or paprika over the peanuts and toss again.
8. Allow the peanuts to cool before serving.

MTORI WA NAZI NA MAHARAGE (BANANA AND COCONUT STEW WITH BEANS)

- **Servings:** 4
- **Time:** 40 minutes

Ingredients:

- 4 ripe bananas, peeled and sliced
- 1 cup cooked beans (black-eyed peas or kidney beans)
- 1 cup coconut milk
- 1 onion, finely chopped
- 2 tomatoes, diced
- 2 tablespoons vegetable oil
- 2 cloves garlic, minced
- 1 teaspoon ginger, grated
- 1 teaspoon ground coriander
- 1/2 teaspoon turmeric powder
- 1/2 teaspoon cayenne pepper (adjust to taste)
- Salt to taste
- Fresh cilantro for garnish

Instructions:

1. In a pan, heat vegetable oil over medium heat. Add chopped onions, minced garlic, and grated ginger. Sauté until onions are soft and translucent.
2. Add diced tomatoes to the pan and cook until they break down and form a thick mixture.
3. Stir in ground coriander, turmeric powder, and cayenne pepper. Cook for an additional 2-3 minutes.
4. Add sliced bananas and cooked beans to the pan, gently stirring to combine with the spice and tomato mixture.
5. Pour coconut milk over the ingredients, ensuring they are well-coated with the flavorful liquid.
6. Season with salt to taste and let the stew simmer for 15-20 minutes, allowing the flavors to meld and the bananas to soften.
7. Garnish with fresh cilantro before serving.

MBOGA YA NAZI NA MAHARAGE (VEGETABLES IN COCONUT SAUCE WITH BEANS)

- **Servings:** 4
- **Time:** 30 minutes

Ingredients:

- 2 cups mixed vegetables (carrots, green beans, peas), chopped
- 1 cup cooked beans (black-eyed peas or kidney beans)
- 1 cup coconut milk
- 1 onion, finely chopped
- 2 tomatoes, diced
- 2 tablespoons vegetable oil
- 2 cloves garlic, minced
- 1 teaspoon ginger, grated
- 1 teaspoon ground coriander
- 1/2 teaspoon turmeric powder
- 1/2 teaspoon cayenne pepper (adjust to taste)
- Salt to taste
- Fresh cilantro for garnish

Instructions:

1. In a pan, heat vegetable oil over medium heat. Add chopped onions, minced garlic, and grated ginger. Sauté until onions are soft and translucent.
2. Add diced tomatoes to the pan and cook until they break down and form a thick mixture.
3. Stir in ground coriander, turmeric powder, and cayenne pepper. Cook for an additional 2-3 minutes.

4. Add mixed vegetables and cooked beans to the pan, stirring to combine with the spice and tomato mixture.
5. Pour coconut milk over the vegetables and beans, ensuring they are well-coated with the flavorful liquid.
6. Season with salt to taste and let the mixture simmer for 15-20 minutes, allowing the vegetables to cook and absorb the coconut-infused flavors.
7. Garnish with fresh cilantro before serving.

MAHARAGE NA WALI (BEANS AND RICE)

- **Servings:** 4
- **Time:** 40 minutes

Ingredients:

- 2 cups cooked beans (black-eyed peas or kidney beans)
- 2 cups basmati rice, washed and drained
- 1 cup coconut milk
- 1 onion, finely chopped
- 2 tomatoes, diced
- 2 tablespoons vegetable oil
- 2 cloves garlic, minced
- 1 teaspoon ginger, grated
- 1 teaspoon ground coriander
- 1/2 teaspoon turmeric powder
- 1/2 teaspoon cayenne pepper (adjust to taste)
- Salt to taste
- Fresh cilantro for garnish

Instructions:

1. In a pot, heat vegetable oil over medium heat. Add chopped onions, minced garlic, and grated ginger. Sauté until onions are soft and translucent.
2. Add diced tomatoes to the pot and cook until they break down and form a thick mixture.
3. Stir in ground coriander, turmeric powder, and cayenne pepper. Cook for an additional 2-3 minutes.
4. Add cooked beans to the pot, mixing well with the spice and tomato mixture.
5. Add washed basmati rice to the pot, stirring to combine with the other ingredients.
6. Pour in coconut milk, ensuring the rice and beans are well-submerged in the liquid.
7. Season with salt to taste and bring the mixture to a boil.
8. Once boiling, reduce the heat to low, cover the pot, and let the rice and beans simmer for 15-20 minutes or until the rice is tender and has absorbed the coconut-infused flavors.
9. Fluff the rice with a fork to separate the grains.
10. Garnish with fresh cilantro before serving.

KAIMATI (SWEET DUMPLINGS)

- **Servings:** 4-6
- **Time:** 1.5 hours (including resting time)

Ingredients:

- 2 cups all-purpose flour
- 1/2 cup sugar
- 1 teaspoon baking powder
- 1/2 teaspoon ground cardamom
- 1/4 teaspoon salt

- 1 cup coconut milk
- Vegetable oil for frying
- 1 cup coconut flakes (optional, for coating)
- Honey or sugar syrup for drizzling

Instructions:

1. In a large bowl, combine the all-purpose flour, sugar, baking powder, ground cardamom, and salt.
2. Gradually add coconut milk to the dry ingredients, stirring continuously to form a smooth, thick batter.
3. Cover the bowl and let the batter rest for at least 1 hour to allow it to rise and develop flavor.
4. In a deep pan, heat vegetable oil over medium heat for frying.
5. Using a spoon or your hands, scoop small portions of the batter and drop them into the hot oil. Fry until the kaimati turn golden brown and are fully cooked inside. Ensure even cooking by turning them occasionally.
6. Once cooked, remove the kaimati from the oil and let them drain on paper towels to absorb excess oil.
7. Optional: Roll the warm kaimati in coconut flakes to coat them for added texture and flavor.
8. Drizzle honey or sugar syrup over the kaimati for a sweet finish.

SWEET ENDINGS

MANDAZI (TANZANIAN DOUGHNUTS)

- **Servings:** 4-6
- **Time:** 1.5 hours (including resting time)

Ingredients:

- 2 cups all-purpose flour
- 1/2 cup sugar
- 1 teaspoon baking powder
- 1/4 teaspoon salt
- 1/2 teaspoon ground cinnamon
- 1/4 teaspoon ground cardamom
- 1/2 cup coconut milk
- 1/4 cup water
- Vegetable oil for frying

Instructions:

1. In a large bowl, combine the all-purpose flour, sugar, baking powder, salt, ground cinnamon, and ground cardamom.
2. In a separate bowl, mix the coconut milk and water.
3. Gradually add the coconut milk mixture to the dry ingredients, stirring continuously to form a soft and non-sticky dough.
4. Knead the dough on a floured surface until it is smooth and elastic.
5. Cover the dough and let it rest for about 30 minutes to allow it to rise.
6. Roll out the dough to a thickness of about 1/2 inch and cut it into desired shapes (squares or triangles).
7. In a deep pan, heat vegetable oil over medium heat for frying.
8. Fry the mandazi in batches until they are golden brown on both sides, ensuring they are fully cooked inside.
9. Once cooked, remove the mandazi from the oil and let them drain on paper towels to absorb excess oil.

MBATATA WA NAZI (COCONUT SWEET POTATOES)

- **Servings:** 4
- **Time:** 40 minutes

Ingredients:

- 2 large sweet potatoes, peeled and sliced
- 1 cup coconut milk
- 1/2 cup sugar

- 1/4 teaspoon ground cinnamon
- 1/4 teaspoon ground cardamom
- 1/4 teaspoon salt
- 2 tablespoons vegetable oil
- Shredded coconut for garnish (optional)

Instructions:

1. In a pot, bring water to a boil and add the sliced sweet potatoes. Boil until they are just tender but still firm. Drain the sweet potatoes and set aside.
2. In a separate bowl, mix together coconut milk, sugar, ground cinnamon, ground cardamom, and salt to create a sweet and spiced coconut mixture.
3. Heat vegetable oil in a pan over medium heat.
4. Add the boiled sweet potatoes to the pan and sauté for a few minutes until they start to brown.
5. Pour the coconut milk mixture over the sweet potatoes, ensuring they are well-coated.
6. Simmer the sweet potatoes in the coconut mixture for about 20-25 minutes or until they are soft and have absorbed the flavors.
7. Stir occasionally to prevent sticking and ensure even coating.
8. Once the sweet potatoes are tender and the coconut milk has thickened into a syrupy consistency, remove from heat.
9. Garnish with shredded coconut if desired.

KASHATA (COCONUT CANDY)

- **Servings:** 8-10
- **Time:** 30 minutes (plus cooling time)

Ingredients:

- 2 cups desiccated coconut
- 1 cup sugar
- 1/2 cup water
- 1/2 teaspoon vanilla extract
- A pinch of salt

Instructions:

1. In a pan, combine sugar and water over medium heat, stirring until the sugar dissolves.
2. Bring the sugar-water mixture to a gentle boil, then reduce the heat to simmer for about 5-7 minutes, creating a simple syrup.
3. Add desiccated coconut to the simple syrup, stirring continuously to combine.
4. Continue cooking the mixture over medium heat, stirring constantly, until it thickens and starts to come away from the sides of the pan.
5. Add vanilla extract and a pinch of salt to enhance the flavor. Stir well.
6. Once the coconut mixture is thick and sticky, remove it from the heat.
7. Grease a flat surface or a tray with a little oil.
8. Pour the coconut mixture onto the greased surface and spread it out evenly to your desired thickness.
9. Allow the coconut mixture to cool for a few minutes, then score it into squares or diamond shapes with a knife.
10. Let the Kashata cool completely before breaking it along the scored lines.

MKATE WA UFUTA (SESAME BREAD)

- **Servings:** 8-10
- **Time:** 2 hours (including rising time)

Ingredients:

- 3 cups all-purpose flour
- 1 tablespoon active dry yeast
- 1 cup warm water
- 2 tablespoons sugar
- 1 teaspoon salt
- 3 tablespoons sesame seeds
- 2 tablespoons vegetable oil
- Additional sesame seeds for sprinkling

Instructions:

1. In a bowl, combine warm water, sugar, and active dry yeast. Let it sit for 5-10 minutes until the mixture becomes frothy.
2. In a large mixing bowl, combine flour and salt.
3. Make a well in the center of the flour mixture and pour in the yeast mixture.
4. Gradually incorporate the flour into the wet ingredients, kneading until a soft and elastic dough forms.
5. Place the dough on a floured surface and knead for about 8-10 minutes until it becomes smooth and springs back when touched.
6. Grease a bowl with vegetable oil, place the dough in it, and cover with a damp cloth. Allow the dough to rise in a warm place for 1 hour or until it doubles in size.
7. Preheat the oven to 375°F (190°C).

8. Punch down the risen dough and knead in sesame seeds.
9. Divide the dough into two equal portions and shape each into a round loaf.
10. Place the loaves on a greased baking sheet, sprinkle additional sesame seeds on top, and let them rise for another 30 minutes.
11. Bake in the preheated oven for 20-25 minutes or until the bread is golden brown and sounds hollow when tapped.
12. Allow the Sesame Bread to cool on a wire rack before slicing.

SUPU YA MABOGA (PUMPKIN SOUP)

- **Servings:** 4
- **Time:** 40 minutes

Ingredients:

- 2 cups pumpkin, peeled and cubed
- 1 onion, chopped
- 2 cloves garlic, minced
- 1 carrot, peeled and chopped
- 1 potato, peeled and chopped
- 4 cups vegetable broth
- 1 cup coconut milk
- 2 tablespoons vegetable oil
- 1 teaspoon ground coriander
- 1/2 teaspoon ground cumin
- Salt and pepper to taste
- Fresh cilantro for garnish

Instructions:

1. In a large pot, heat vegetable oil over medium heat. Add chopped onions and minced garlic. Sauté until onions are soft and translucent.
2. Add ground coriander and ground cumin to the pot. Stir well to coat the onions and garlic in the spices.
3. Add chopped pumpkin, carrot, and potato to the pot, stirring to combine with the spice mixture.
4. Pour in vegetable broth, ensuring the vegetables are well-submerged. Bring the mixture to a boil.
5. Once boiling, reduce the heat to low, cover the pot, and let the vegetables simmer for 20-25 minutes or until they are tender.
6. Use an immersion blender to puree the soup until smooth. Alternatively, transfer the soup to a blender in batches, blend, and return to the pot.
7. Stir in coconut milk, salt, and pepper. Simmer for an additional 5-10 minutes.
8. Adjust the seasoning according to taste.
9. Garnish with fresh cilantro before serving.

BISKUTI YA NAZI (COCONUT COOKIES)

- **Servings:** 20 cookies
- **Time:** 30 minutes

Ingredients:

- 1 cup all-purpose flour
- 1 cup desiccated coconut
- 1/2 cup sugar
- 1/2 cup unsalted butter, softened
- 1 teaspoon vanilla extract
- A pinch of salt

Instructions:

1. Preheat the oven to 350°F (180°C) and line a baking sheet with parchment paper.
2. In a bowl, cream together the softened butter and sugar until light and fluffy.
3. Add vanilla extract to the butter-sugar mixture and mix well.
4. In a separate bowl, combine the all-purpose flour, desiccated coconut, and a pinch of salt.
5. Gradually add the dry ingredients to the butter mixture, mixing until a soft dough forms.
6. Take small portions of the dough and roll them into balls. Place the balls on the prepared baking sheet, leaving space between each for spreading.
7. Flatten each ball slightly with the back of a fork or your fingers.
8. Bake in the preheated oven for 12-15 minutes or until the edges of the cookies turn golden brown.
9. Allow the cookies to cool on the baking sheet for a few minutes before transferring them to a wire rack to cool completely.

MKATE WA BANANA (BANANA BREAD)

- **Servings:** 8-10 slices
- **Time:** 1 hour

Ingredients:

- 3 ripe bananas, mashed
- 1/2 cup unsalted butter, melted
- 1 teaspoon vanilla extract

- 1/2 cup sugar
- 1 large egg, beaten
- 1 1/2 cups all-purpose flour
- 1 teaspoon baking soda
- A pinch of salt
- 1/2 cup chopped nuts or chocolate chips (optional)

Instructions:

1. Preheat the oven to 350°F (180°C). Grease a loaf pan and set it aside.
2. In a large mixing bowl, mash the ripe bananas with a fork.
3. Melt the butter and add it to the mashed bananas along with the vanilla extract. Mix well.
4. Add the sugar and beaten egg to the banana mixture, stirring until well combined.
5. In a separate bowl, whisk together the flour, baking soda, and a pinch of salt.
6. Gradually add the dry ingredients to the banana mixture, stirring until just combined. Be careful not to overmix.
7. If desired, fold in chopped nuts or chocolate chips for added texture and flavor.
8. Pour the batter into the prepared loaf pan, spreading it evenly.
9. Bake in the preheated oven for 50-60 minutes or until a toothpick inserted into the center comes out clean.
10. Allow the Banana Bread to cool in the pan for 10 minutes before transferring it to a wire rack to cool completely.

MEASUREMENT CONVERSIONS

Volume Conversions:

- 1 cup = 8 fluid ounces = 240 milliliters
- 1 tablespoon = 3 teaspoons = 15 milliliters
- 1 fluid ounce = 2 tablespoons = 30 milliliters
- 1 quart = 4 cups = 32 fluid ounces = 946 milliliters
- 1 gallon = 4 quarts = 128 fluid ounces = 3.78 liters
- 1 liter = 1,000 milliliters = 33.8 fluid ounces
- 1 milliliter = 0.034 fluid ounces = 0.002 cups

Weight Conversions:

- 1 pound = 16 ounces = 453.592 grams
- 1 ounce = 28.349 grams
- 1 gram = 0.035 ounces = 0.001 kilograms
- 1 kilogram = 1,000 grams = 35.274 ounces = 2.205 pounds

Temperature Conversions:

- To convert from Fahrenheit to Celsius: (°F - 32) / 1.8
- To convert from Celsius to Fahrenheit: (°C * 1.8) + 32

Length Conversions:

- 1 inch = 2.54 centimeters
- 1 foot = 12 inches = 30.48 centimeters
- 1 yard = 3 feet = 36 inches = 91.44 centimeters
- 1 meter = 100 centimeters = 1.094 yards.

Made in the USA
Columbia, SC
16 March 2025